Cigar Bizarre

CIGAR BIZARRE

AN UNUSUAL HISTORY

PHILIP COLLINS

PHOTOGRAPHY BY DAN SUNDSTROM

GPG

GENERAL
PUBLISHING
GROUP, INC

Publisher: W. Quay Hays
Editorial Director: Peter L. Hoffman
Designer: Robert Avellan
Special artworks: Frank Cardoza
Production Director: Trudihope Schlomowitz
Color and Prepress Manager: Bill Castillo
Production Artist: Gaston Moraga
Production Assistants: Tom Archibeque, David Chadderdon, Russel Lockwood, Roy Penn, Regina Troyer
Editorial Assistant: Dana Stibor

A Fillip Book
Photo composition and art direction: Philip Collins

For information:
General Publishing Group, Inc.
2701 Ocean Park Boulevard, Suite 140
Santa Monica, CA 90405

Library of Congress Cataloging-in-Publication Data

Collins, Philip, 1944-
    Cigar bizarre : an unusual history / by Philip Collins ; photography by Dan Sundstrom.
        p.   cm.
    ISBN 1-57544-067-9 (pbk.)
    1. Cigars-Social aspects. 2. Cigars-History. 3. Cigars-Humor.
    I. Title.
    GT3020.C58   1997
    394.1'4-dc21   97-23856
                                                            CIP

Printed in the USA by RR Donnelley & Sons Company
10 9 8 7 6 5 4 3 2 1

General Publishing Group
Los Angeles

Dedicated to the memory of Nat Cohen, a man who knew his cigars and how to enjoy his money.

Contents

Introduction

After 6,000 years of enlightenment, the human race has arrived at a point where there is universal agreement on one thing and one thing only: that the tobacco growers and tobacco purveyors, under their sinister cloaks and secret cabals, are the new Princes of Darkness. Their unstated but unilaterally understood mission to poison the world with their evil products is now clear to all right-thinking people and they, and the unfortunates they have skillfully manipulated to become "users" (smokers), are our demons and new pariahs in today's politically correct social order. That the human race has survived the onslaught of the last 100 years of brainwashing, seductive advertising, penal taxation (if you are a 'user'), attractive vending machines and media idols blowing smoke at us from our TV and cinema screens is nothing short of a miracle. God be praised. The prairie we knew as Marlboro Country has become the Village of the Damned. Where to go? What to do? How to think?

For some time now, probably as long as an eon or two, one tobacco product has survived the slings and arrows, brickbats and poisoned pens of the outraged to become an institution in cultured and polite society, and a source of extreme pleasure for the rest of us. I speak of the noble cigar.

That the cigar has generated little controversy weighs heavily in favor of the tacit acceptance and affectionate approval it has enjoyed throughout the ages. Few would question the sagacity of Sir Winston Churchill or George Burns, two of the planet's most prodigious puffers.

There is a mountain of information and little remembered history about the cigar which, although known to the two aforementioned worthies, needs, in the opinion of a new generation of aficionados, particular and serious attention.

Hence *Cigar Bizarre.*

Henry Ford, well known for his mass-produced cars, and less applauded for his virulent anti-Semitism and proclamation that "History is bunk," may have had a point (concerning the latter, I hasten to add). But, if history has taught us anything, it has advised us to entertain a skeptical thought or two. Whether history is "an excitable and lying old lady," according to Guy de Maupassant, or "incomprehensible without Jesus," according to Ernest Renon, history has its place in, well...history.

Hence *Cigar Bizarre.*

Throughout the vast spectrum of social, artistic, inventive and creative endeavor, the cigar has been in evidence. From the birth of the Pyramids through 5,000 years to NASA experiments in outer space, the cigar has played its part. That the cigar was smoked in the early dynasties of Aztec and Inca noblemen and by men of God does not negate the possibility that cigars were rolled and smoked by ancestry through the wandering tribes of Israel back to Eden and the first man. Earliest documented references to cigar smoking are, however, confined to religious ceremony in pre-Conquistador days on the South American continent. It is probable that these local blends contained elements more commonly associated with mind-altering properties than the regular benign smoke of today's popular brands. However, smoking is but one use of the multifaceted stogie.

Hence *Cigar Bizarre.*

When the English explorer Sir Walter Raleigh introduced tobacco to the Western world in 1595, he claimed his finding as an historic first for England, only to be upstaged in 1922 by the discovery of the oldest existing cigar buried alongside King Tutankhamen with a hoard of other collectibles from 1358 B.C. The fascinating theory of Dr. Hans Klopfer, the eminent Austrian biochemist, whose conjecture that the great pyramids were in fact prefabricated and rolled to their current locations on an immense relay of specially rolled cigars, is supported by the discovery of the cigar at the young king's final resting place. "You are what you smoke" is a rough translation of a set of hieroglyphs discovered over the sarcophagus of the boy king.

Influences on the course of world history do not end with the ancient Egyptians. Stunning evidence, in the form of original drawings and diagrams on papyrus, indicates that the Wooden Horse of Troy was originally conceived as a giant humidor to carry the magnanimous gift of 500,000 Prima Bellicosas #4 to the Trojans to lull them into a sense of false security.

The world of transport owes a debt of homage to the cigar for its influences on the streamlined, aerodynamic shaping of automobiles and dirigibles during the early 20th century. Great artists including Leonardo da Vinci and René Magritte would happily acknowledge the inspiration of the cigar in major works, were they painting today. Indeed, in his landmark biography *A Life of Leaves,* Ramon Cortez makes a reasoned argument for the cigar as being not only the inspiration but the mainstay and raison d'être for many artistic talents who survived poverty all their working days, only to become rich in posthumous celebrity.

Phallic symbolism and sensual textural qualities have added to the mystique and affection of the cigar among the gentler sex. Formally viewed as the prerogative of the affluent male, cigar enjoyment has now flooded across the gender frontier. No longer do dinner parties conclude with the gentlemen retiring to one room to enjoy their cigars and discuss important affairs of state while the ladies are left to chatter among themselves. The distaff nobility now indulge decision-making discussion while toting a Panatela or even a chubby Robusto in board rooms and cocktail lounges from coast to coast. Indeed, tobacco sexing and blending at home (see page 27) is now the fastest-growing fashion in the kitchens of Anytown, USA, for those who prefer to roll their own. Can cigar soireés for the Tupperware set be far behind? Not when we consider the changing role of the Avon Lady. We can count the days to a time when a full range of Lady Cigars will be on hand for the shop-at-home housewife. "Ding Dong! Suzie Cigar calling!"

With myriad social attributes to its credit, the cigar continues to be a source of inspiration to artists and artisans and, incredibly, original thinkers in all aspects of technology and space exploration. Expect the introduction of the digital cigar before next year's tobacco crop is harvested. A smokeless stogie for the ecologically challenged will put to rest any fears of polluting the fragile ozone balance. Self-igniting cigars will save a million trees a year. Matches will be confined to museums and curiosity shops.

As sophisticated and diverse in its uses as the cigar proclaims, there exists, however, consternation in the Rand Corporation and covert agencies around the world. It is simply that no extraterrestrial has ever been depicted, seen or photographed with a cigar. This anomaly is the subject of heated debate among UFOlogists and others confined to institutions for the paranormal.

As we enter the 21st century, it is only now that we are beginning to understand the ritual role of the cigar in religion, particularly the ancient variety: Druids, Zealots, Rastafarians and beyond. A good puff before a weekly human sacrifice or the summoning of a plague was quite probable, according to Archdeacon Madison Arnold. It was Arnold who discovered the Shroud of Montecristo among looted Nazi war treasures in post-WWII Germany. Now returned to its native island of Cuba, the shroud, purporting to resemble the shadow and logo of the legendary Montecristo Excellento, is said to glow red at its tip on every Sunday during Lent. Other extraordinary phenomena are presented in the following pages, both contemporary and historical.

It was Oliver Wendell Holmes Jr. who stated in 1921, "A page of history is worth a volume of logic."

Hence, *Cigar Bizarre.*

"Cigars? Cigars and wine have one thing in common.
The Niagara of bullshit that is written about them."
—*Henri de Villeneuve*

Transportation

ENGINE NACELLE
OIL TANK
FRESH WATER TANK

OBSERVATION WINDOWS
DINING SALON
PROVISIONS

WATER

MAIL ROOM
BALLAS T TANK

AIR TANK

156.5

MAIL ROOM

FREIG HT
ROOM

TANK

203.0

10   11   12   13   14
16.5   16.5   15   15   15
            15

LARGE FREIGHT ROOM
ENGINE NACELLE

RADIO ROOM
PASSENGER STATEROOM
DINING SALON
OBSERVATION WINDOWS

Before the introduction of Combustarosa Especiales as power-drive convection engines, the Zeppelin airships would blow up with boring regularity.

"...so Jim took up some of the top planks of the raft and built a snug wigwam to get under in blazing weather and rainy, to keep things dry."

—The Adventures of Huckleberry Finn

Towards the end of the 19th century, when steam-driven engineering was all the rage, skeptical shipping-line owners tested the waters with Super Colossalarosas as a power source while maintaining full-sail rigging aboard their quality ships. Pioneered by the Swiss Navy, the huge bellows employed to "smoke-drive" the vessels often exhaled sufficient air currents to activate the mighty canvas rigging and speed the ship to meet a contracted delivery deadline.

Before John Cobb attempted the world's land speed record in 1938 on the Bonneville Salt Flats, he conducted numerous tests in aerodynamics, stability and fuel safety under simulated conditions. A specially constructed Torpedo Immenso was put through its paces on a newly laid salt track. The resultant success was clearly recognized. Note the streamlined torpedo design influences on the actual car that achieved the world record.

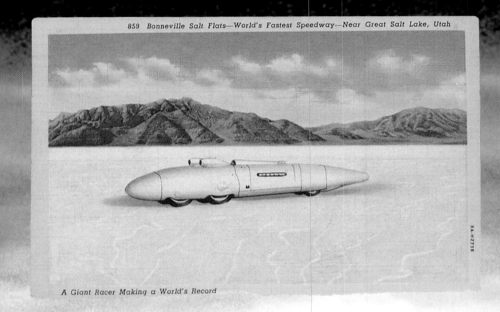

859 Bonneville Salt Flats—World's Fastest Speedway—Near Great Salt Lake, Utah

A Giant Racer Making a World's Record

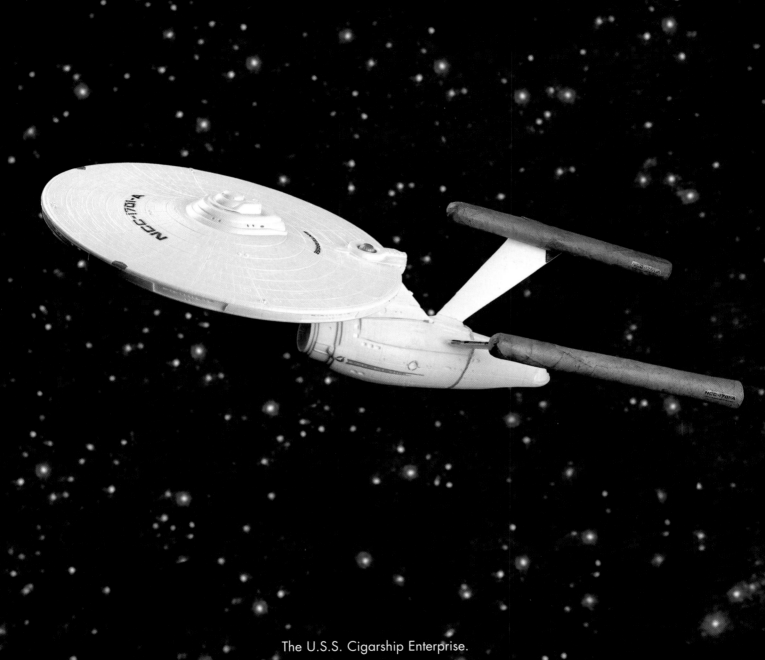

The U.S.S. Cigarship Enterprise.

THE SMOKING EXPERIENCE

In the early 1900s, rolling cigars by hand became an art form of calisthenics for the midget ladies of Camagüey.

The mystique surrounding the process of tobacco blending is explained: Anyone with a blender and a supply of electricity can do the job.

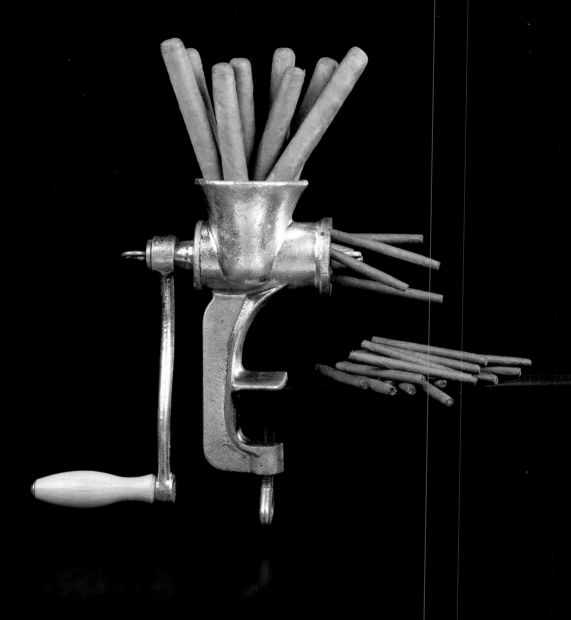

After his operation, Mr. Simon Potz of Schenectady, New York, could only smoke small cigars. He adapted his meat grinder to transform his cache of priceless aged Havanas into smokes of a convenient size. Patented in 1937, the design remains a classic that has never been improved upon.

Corona Schwartzos are a unique brand of smoke whose wrappers are individually tanned to perfection.

In England during WWII, civilians were exhorted to "Dig for Victory" (plant a vegetable garden). This surviving example of English enterprise was grown by Mr. Arthur Scroggins of Epsom, Surrey, and donated to Sir Winston Churchill on VE Day. The two handsome Churchills, grown in the shape of a "V" for "Victory," are on permanent exhibition in Patriot's Corner at the Imperial War Museum in London.

Another bumper crop of Cuban-seed Coronas and Double Coronas from the tobacco tree of Dr. Louis Fantasia, a cigar blender from San Jose, Costa Rica. The cigars in the upper branches (see inset) are allowed to mature "on the vine" for many years, enhancing their flavor and value.

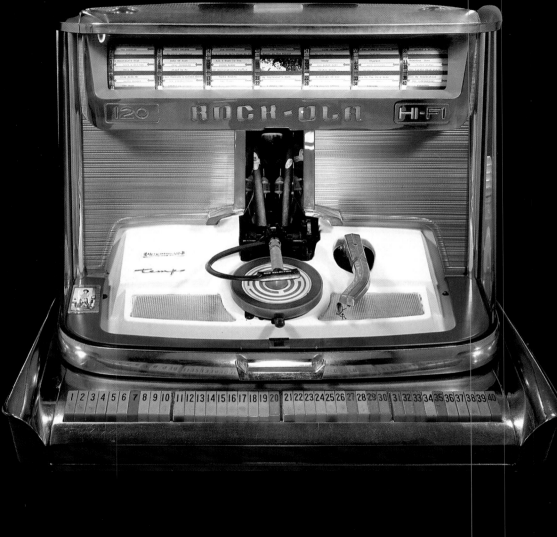

When Harry Rock-ola introduced his new model Hi-Fi Jukebox in 1959, no one could have foreseen the overnight boom in stereo systems that rendered the model obsolete. Like many others, this hi-fi set underwent conversion to an electric humidor with 60 automatic selections.

Whenever cigar aficionados congregate, conversation invariably turns
to ring size, and bragging rights often replace sensible debate.

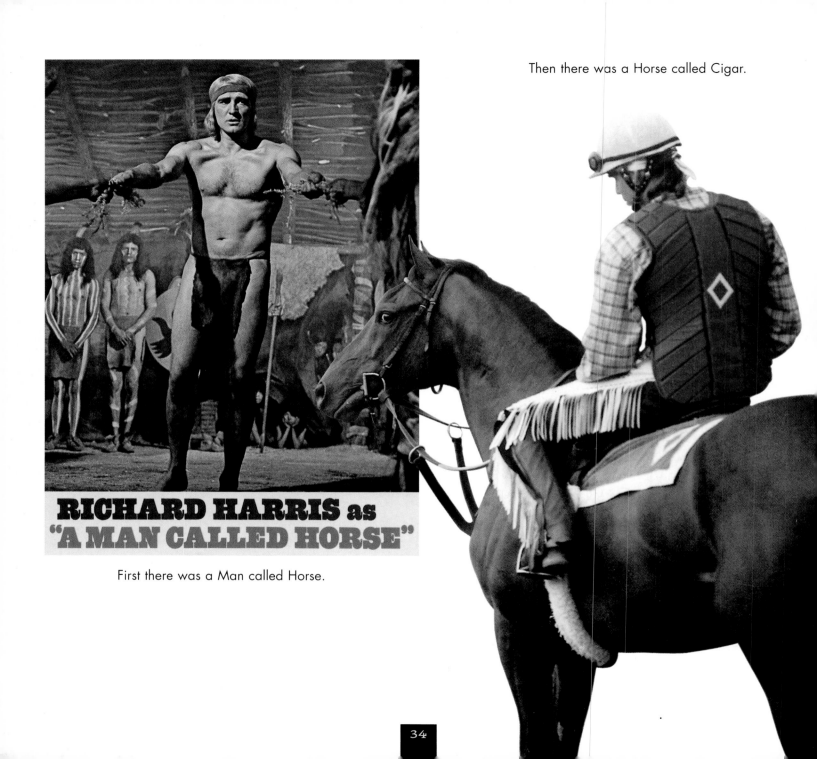

Then there was a Horse called Cigar.

RICHARD HARRIS as
"A MAN CALLED HORSE"

First there was a Man called Horse.

Then there was a Cigar called Horse.

ltimate experience for the smoker with the midnight mun
e magnetic cigars are specially designed for the late
e raider. Just peel off your favorite smoke without the g
opening the fridge door.

What do Michael Milken, Dan Rostenkowski and Charles Keating have in common? They all served out their prison terms in the Brown Bar Hotel, a minimum security establishment where rich and powerful convicted felons may puff on their cigars of choice at any time.

What the hip lawyer/corporate raider/Wall Street bandit is wearing this season.

The age-old great debate is finally solved. Whether a cigar should be smoked with the band in place or removed has long puzzled experts in social graces. Dr. Emil Halbundhalb has patented the ultimate in compromise, the "Demiband." Held in Position A, the band appears present, but turn the cigar 180 degrees and presto!— no band (B). The half-banded cigars (C) are a huge success among the undecided.

All that remains of Professor J. Cornelius Smiley, beloved CEO of the Happy Gag Novelty Company, after the first and only experiment with his new invention—the exploding cigar. His shoes were later bronzed and displayed at the World of Magic in Illusion, Kentucky.

Art & Literature

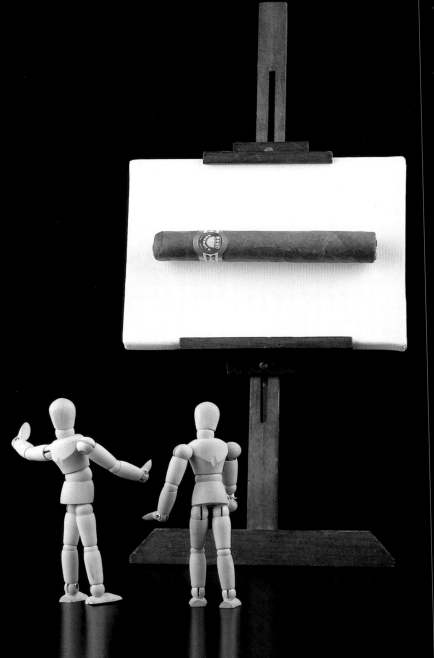

The two critics agreed: It was a work of great importance by a new genius.

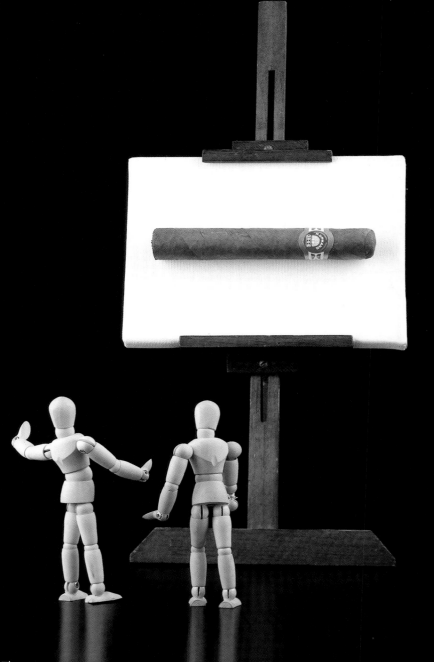

The two critics agreed: It was a work of absolutely no artistic merit whatsoever.

(Acknowledgment: Glen Baxter)

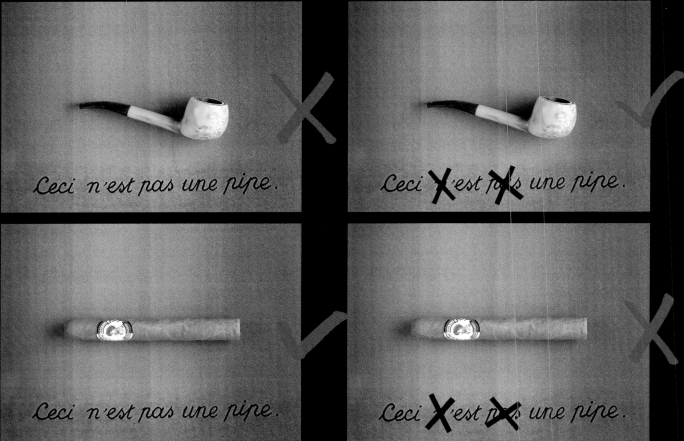

Ceci n'est pas une pipe.

magritte

When embarking on his new masterwork, *This is Not a Pipe*, the Belgian surrealist Rene Magritte enlisted the help of friends to assist him with his faltering command of French. They produced an elaborate selection of visual aids (see page 46), all of which were rejected by the great man in favor of this final version. Une grande erreur.

Ceci n'est pas un cigare.

Magritte explained. How the famous surrealist achieved his vision.

For an April Fool's gag, Michelangelo created two Adams on the ceiling of the Sistine Chapel supporting a giant Corona Religeosa. On April 2, after everyone had enjoyed a good laugh, he over-painted the cigar and the second Adam with God.

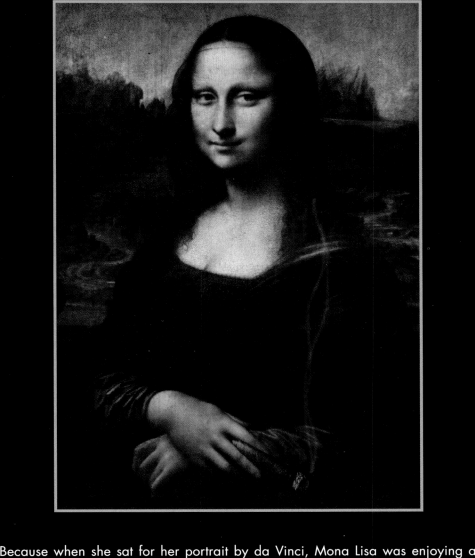

Because when she sat for her portrait by da Vinci, Mona Lisa was enjoying a Fiorntino #3. Polite society in Florence was so enraged, that pressure was brought to bear on the artist by the Anti-tobaccalario League in Milan to erase the smoldering cigar. Leonardo agreed to erase the cigar, but not the smile that resulted from it.

Chapter Uno

Once upon a tyme there was a farm on the southernmost tip of the Cuban island of Cuba. It was built by Jining Cricketta in the year of our Lord 1836 and was blessed with fertile soil and rain in abundance. The natural environment spurred the growth of premium tobacco leaf was normally to be found in the northern peninsula. This persuaded investors to finance location would yield equal to the annual harvest equal to the growers in the north, in volume of bushels, while being superior in size and texture. One of the local farmers whose name

In his landmark literary triumph, *Leaves of Heaven*, there is no reference to the fact that the author, Fernando Miranda, used a cigar pen to write the entire original manuscript. Considered to be the definitive history of tobacco, the book was subsequently translated into 67 languages. Miranda penned all 67 versions with his refillable Plumatanta Double Corona, using only the finest brown tobacco-leaf ink.

The black box journey recorder was discovered some hours later to reveal the last words of the Little Engine's driver: "I think I can! I think I can! I...aaarrrrrgh!"

ARCHITECTURE & MONUMENTS

Not far from Cisbury Ring in Olde Englande is the weather-worn monument, Stogiehenge. It was built by the Druids in ancient times to honor the cigar solstice, when everybody in the surrounding villages would light up to celebrate the longest day.

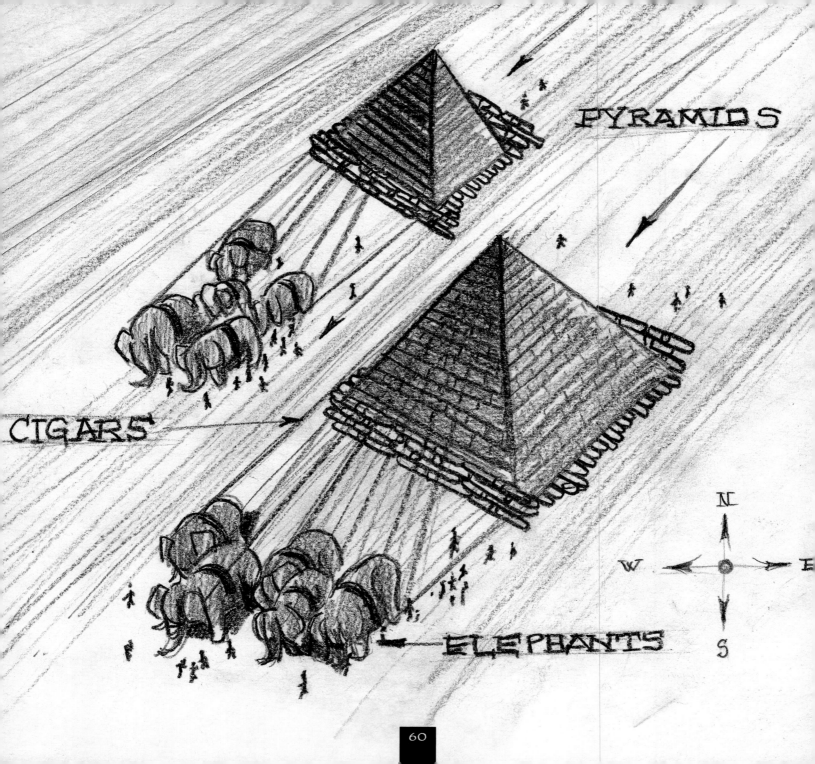

PYRAMIDS

CIGARS

ELEPHANTS

N
W   E
S

60

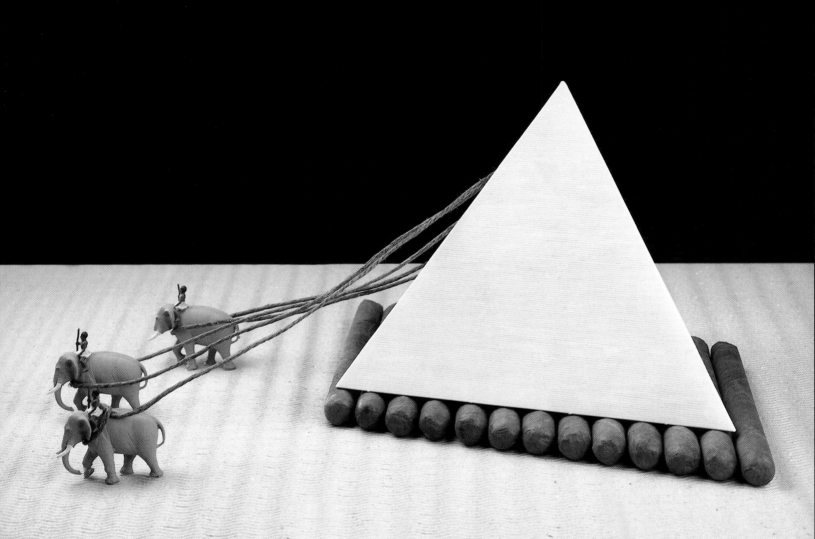

The mystery of the Pyramids solved! Prefabricated at the granite mines, hundreds of miles to the north, the Great Pyramids of Egypt were rolled to their designated locations on a continuous line of Robusto Rollarosas, which were on special order from the young King Hopnotochituk.

The giant sunken cigars of Montezuma, Mexico, predate the prehistoric statues of Easter Island by hundreds, and probably thousands, of years. As with the stone statues, very little is known of their origin, but modern thought suggests a sacred area where cigar smoking was permitted could have been the primary reason for this ancient monument.

When Dioti Salvi designed the Leaning Cigar of Pisa, he did not foresee the consequence of building on soft, alluvial ground. The bell tower, built sometime later to arrest the progressive incline of the cigar, is the only remaining architectural evidence of its monumental presence. The cigar was demolished in 1874 after centuries of eroding stability, leaving the tower to lean at a full 10 degrees out of true as a result of the cigar's continual pressure.

The Clinton White House.

SOCIAL PHENOMENA

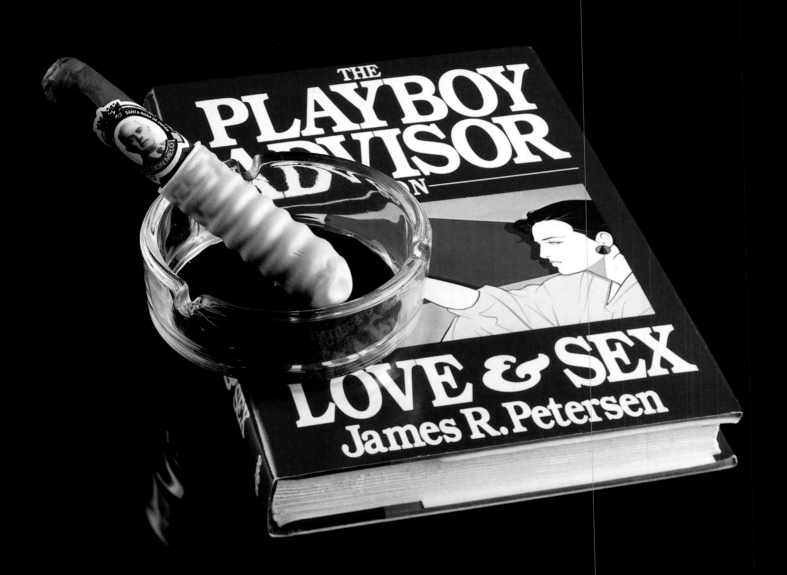

After the Kinsey Report, life was not the same for many brands, which were subjected to 'sensitivity testing' before being given ATF approval for sale to the general public.

Charles Empire-State created his idea for a single stogie humidor in the late 1920s.
The design was later adapted as a blueprint for a tall building in New York.

Designer Workouts for the executive on the move. These handy five-pound weights are considered a must for the discriminating smoker. Available in Robusto, Corona, Churchill and an outsize Double Immensa.

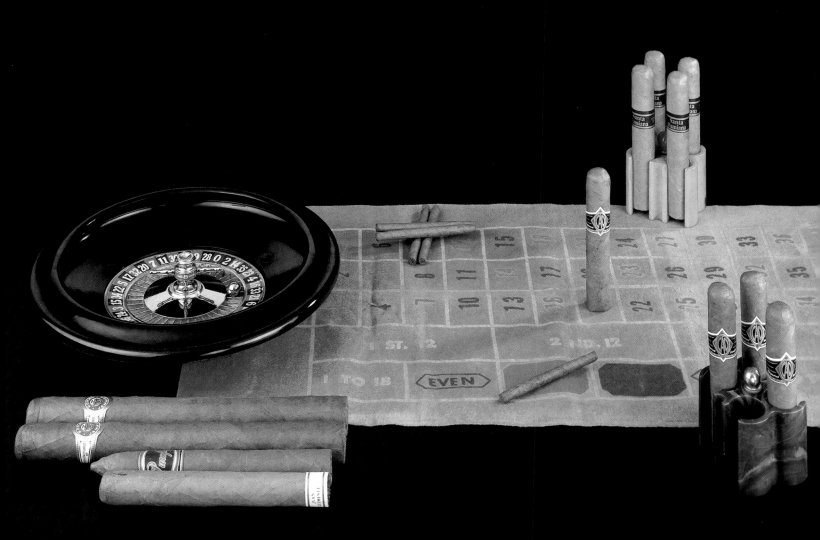

On the Barbary Coast in the mid-1800s, when men were men, cigars were the currency of the roulette wheel...no cheap plastic markers for the playboy pirates of the Pacific. The Humongalosas Rediculosas pictured close to the wheel were the House's guarantee that any bet could be covered.

Before electricity, and even before television, candles were used for illumination and religious ceremony. Before candles, it is probable that cigars served the purpose, and gave their shape to the candle when they became too expensive to function as a mere light source.

In the 1940s and early '50s, Boy Scouts were encouraged to practice their log-sawing skills at summer camp on mighty Churchill #14s before graduating to lumberjack badge status. Girl Scouts were trained to wave flags at each other.

In times gone by, an elite group of artisans honed cigars to specific shapes, according to taste, for the crowned heads of Europe. The monument honoring this now extinct group has recently undergone a multimillion-dollar facelift to provide a brighter tourist attraction in downtown Havana.

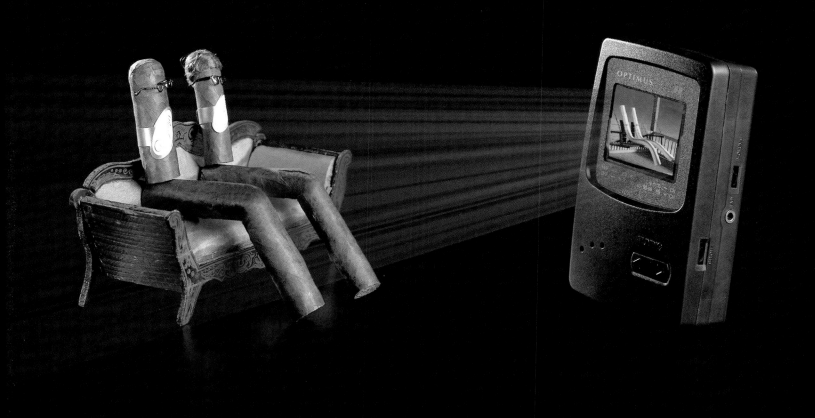

Couch Cigars.

La Fiesta di Circulare is celebrated on April 1st of every year in Honduras as a homage to the local cigar band artisans. Originally created by the leaf growers of Tegucigalpa, this 100-foot animated montage is activated every year in the town square throughout the day-long celebration of the "cherubic" craftspersons.

Practice makes perfect, as any surgeon in the art of circumcision will tell you.
Novices are encouraged to practice on Schlongarosas (#3, 4 and 5).

The small town of Schweinhund lives up to its reputation as the cruelest town in Germany. Every year, on May 1, the smallest of the vertically challenged are dragged from their places of work and forced to walk the slippery cigar over a bath of icky goo, for the delight of the townsfolk. Those who fall off are made to do it again next year.

HISTORY—ANCIENT & MODERN

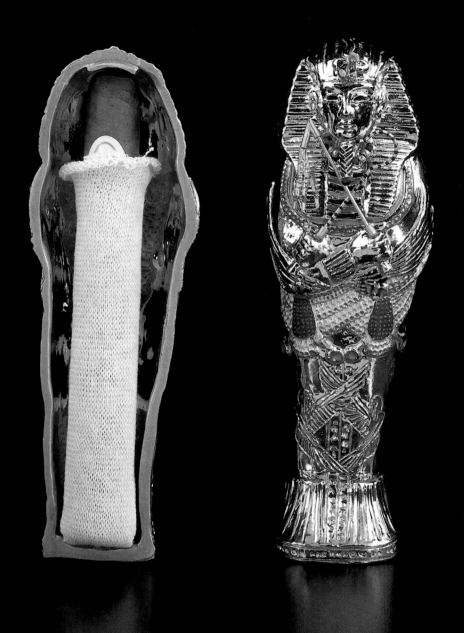

The earliest known example of the cigar, c.1358 B.C. The embalmed form of the Egypto Grosso #4 was discovered next to the solid gold sarcophagus of the Pharaoh Tutankhamen. The Boy King was buried alongside a few thousand of his favorite things.

"The Boy Child appeared indifferent to gold and frankincense, but when he caught sight of the mountain of Gloriosa Habanarosas, his little eyes lit up and he waved his arms excitedly. Here indeed was a wise king."

—*Lithuanians Chapter 4, Verse 5*

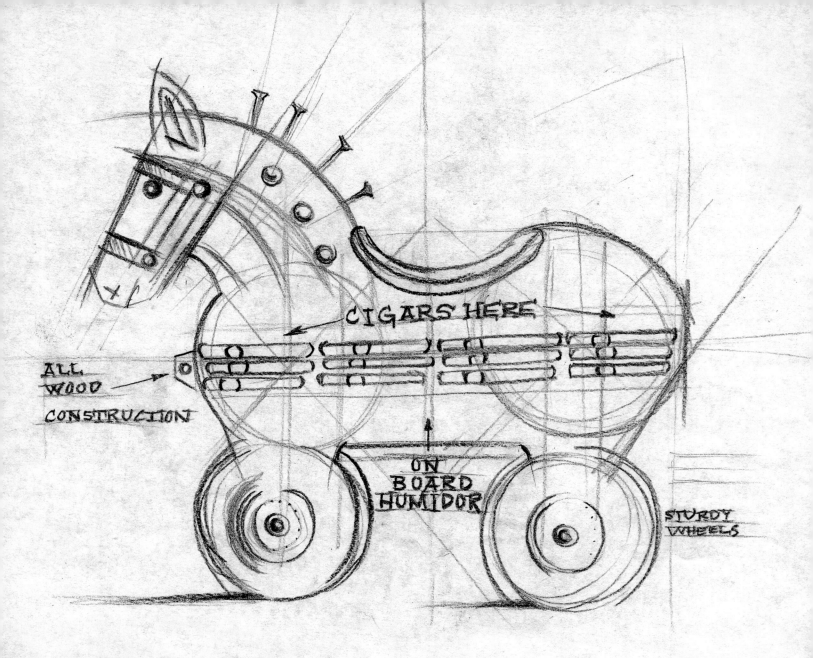

CIGARS HERE

ALL
WOOD
CONSTRUCTION

ON
BOARD
HUMIDOR

STURDY
WHEELS

84

At the start of the siege of Troy in 1193 B.C., Agamemnon ordered the first wooden horse of Troy to be filled with Prima Bellicosas #4, in the hope that the Trojans would think that the Greeks were their pals. It didn't work, and the siege dragged on for 10 years before Ulysses suggested the horse trick again—this time with an elite troop of warriors inside, who succeeded in burning the city to ashes.

An ancient Greek timepiece, the 48-hour cigar clock of Antioch predates Timex by a few thousand years. The ashes that collected in the receptacle were considered sacred as 'evidence of the passage of time,' and sold to the wealthy, who offered them to the gods to 'buy' more time in the hereafter.

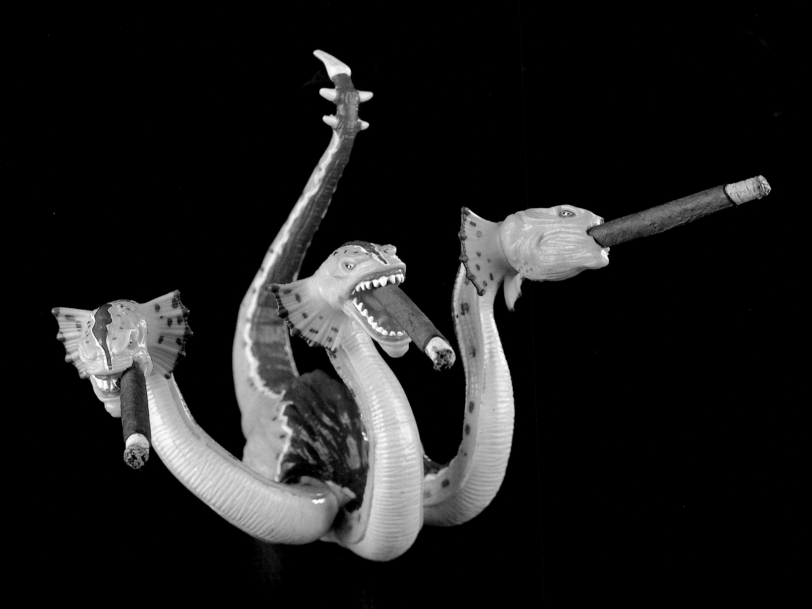

When taking a break from wreaking havoc, the three-headed Hydra agrees with itself that there's nothing like a cool puff to take off the pressure. The Hydra's cigars renew themselves automatically when smoked down to the stub.

The simple Campesinos puffed contentedly on their Enormales, unaware of the arrival of the Obengruppenführer's elite 'clean air' corps, who were renowned for their stealth and sense of fair play.

Sports, Leisure & Theatre

Every year, in the Highland Games, brave Scotsmen competed in "Tossing the Caber," a sport designed to prove who can throw a big pole farthest. Now, in more cultured times, this Highland fling is performed with specially rolled McTavish Monsterosos.

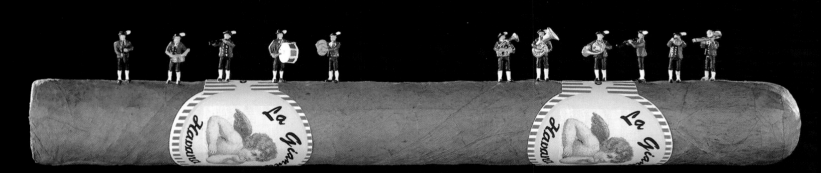

Cigar bands.

When they are not smoking their favorite brands, The Three Aging Tenors prefer to sing old standards like "By the Light of the Silvery Moon," "Sweet Adeline" and "Down by the Old Mill Stream."

"Say 'goodnight,' Gracie."

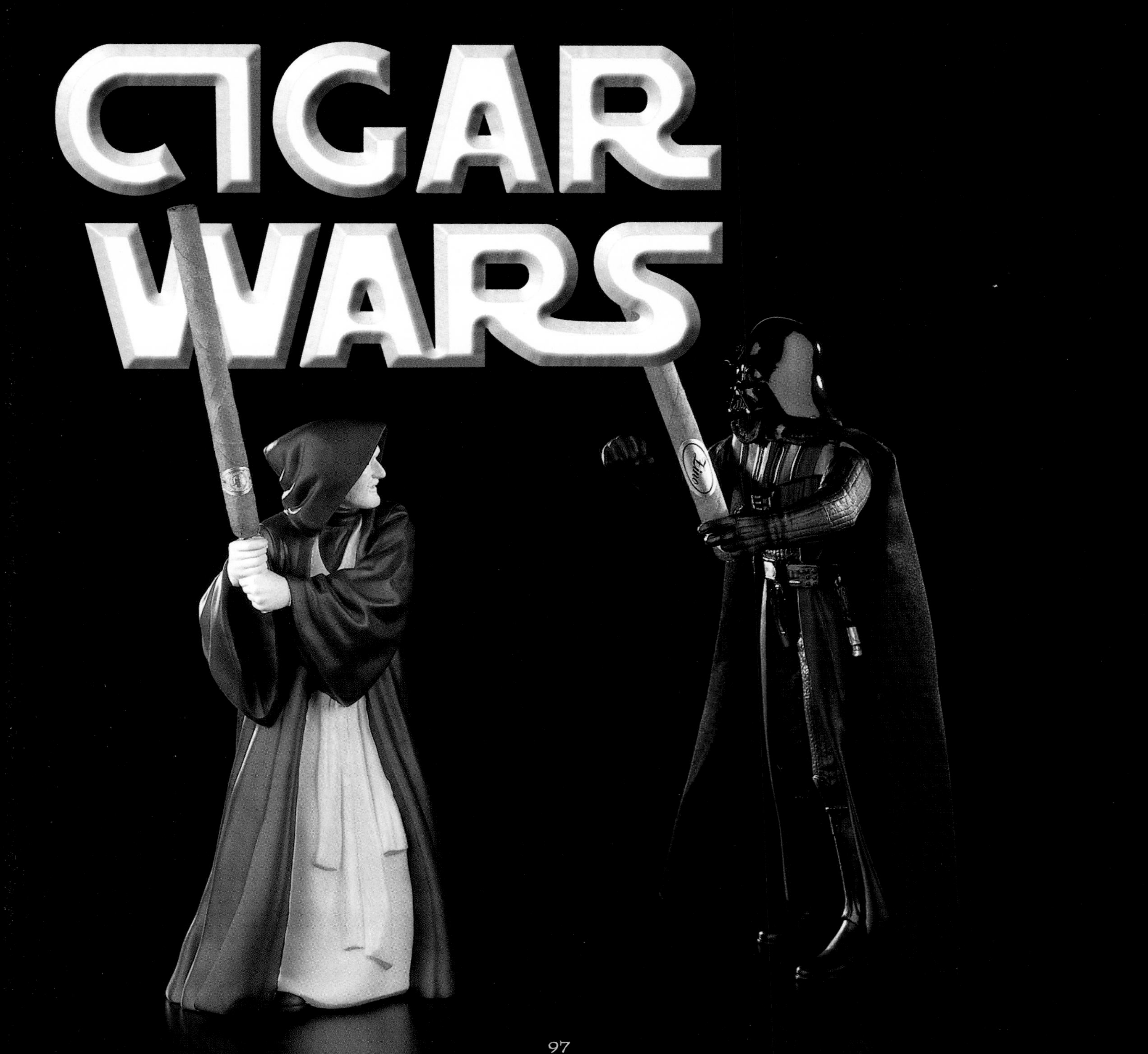
CIGAR
WARS
Zino

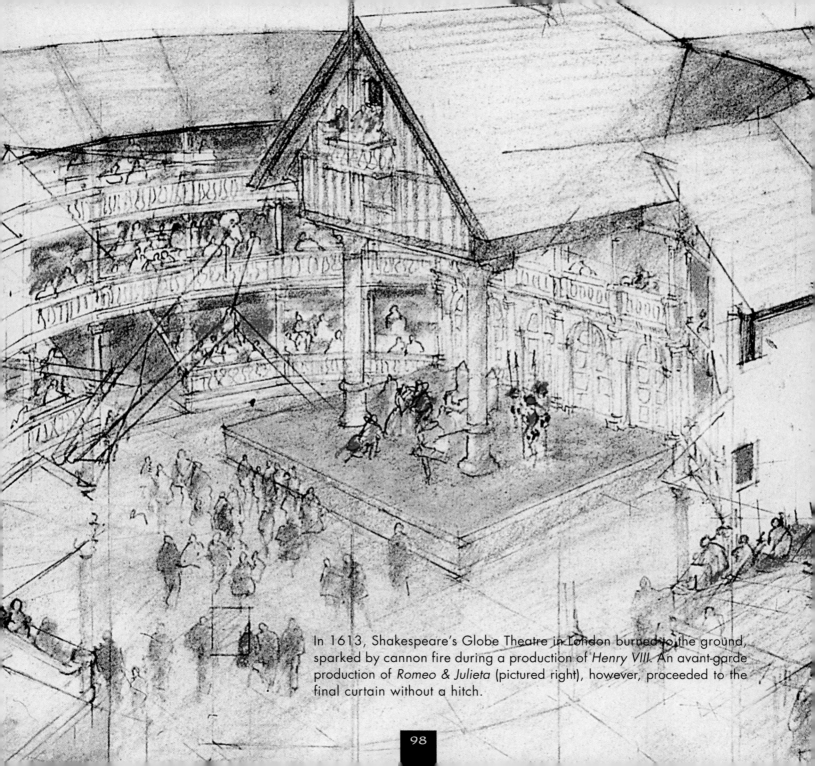

In 1613, Shakespeare's Globe Theatre in London burned to the ground, sparked by cannon fire during a production of *Henry VIII*. An avant-garde production of *Romeo & Julieta* (pictured right), however, proceeded to the final curtain without a hitch.

"Romeo, Romeo, wherefore art thou Romeo?"
"Over here, Julieta, behind the curtain."

From the play *Romeo y Julieta*
By William Shakespeare

THE UNEXPLAINED

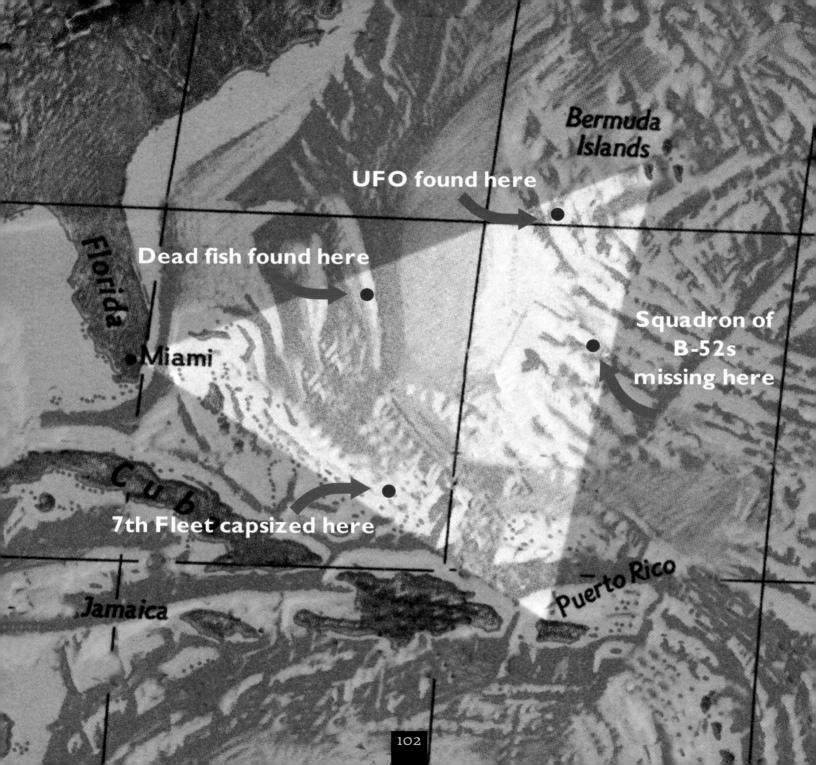

Bermuda Islands

UFO found here

Dead fish found here

Florida

Miami

Squadron of B-52s missing here

Cuba

7th Fleet capsized here

Puerto Rico

Jamaica

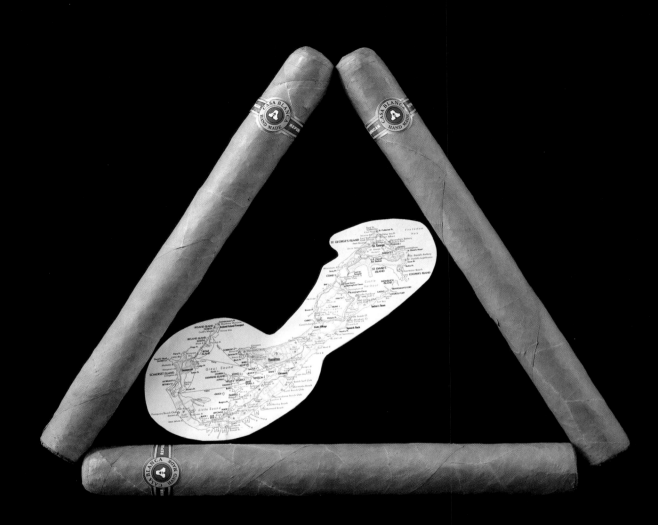

The geography of the island of Bermuda resembles a giant phallus and scrotum, but this has little to do with the curious number of aircraft and ships that go missing in the triangle around it. A recent, popular theory for the strange disappearances is based on the high proportion of cigar smokers on the island who create gigantic pockets of unstable air as they exhale, producing unexpected currents and undertow in the seas around the island.

The newly discovered constellation, Cigarrus Nova, can best be seen in the Western hemisphere during September and October. The brightest stars in this galaxy are Alpha Montecristo, Beta Partagas and Gamma Cohiba. Situated to the right of Ursa Major, the tip of the constellation can sometimes be seen to expel powerful clouds of unidentified gasses.

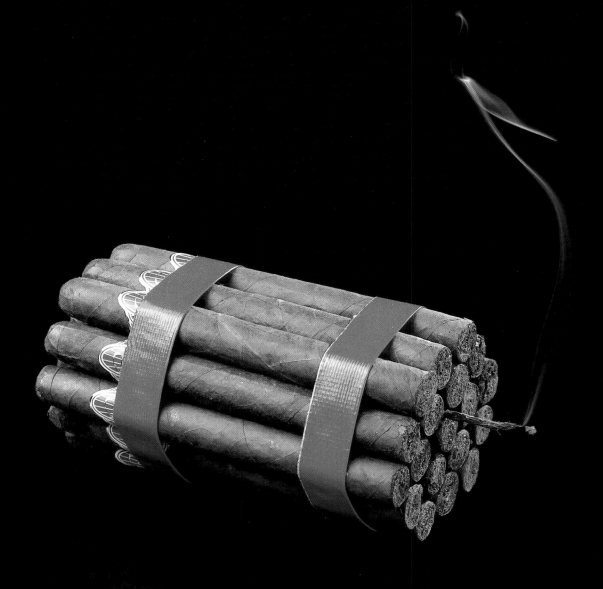

While the Hole in the Wall Gang hogged the headlines across the wild west for their daring heists, little is known of the Shot in the Foot Gang, who were caught red-handed when their dynamite failed to explode. A novice in the art of robbery, the Moondance Kid mistook his cigars for explosives. When the gang was captured, the local sheriff and his posse lit up and smoked the evidence, leaving the gang to go free and foul up several more times.

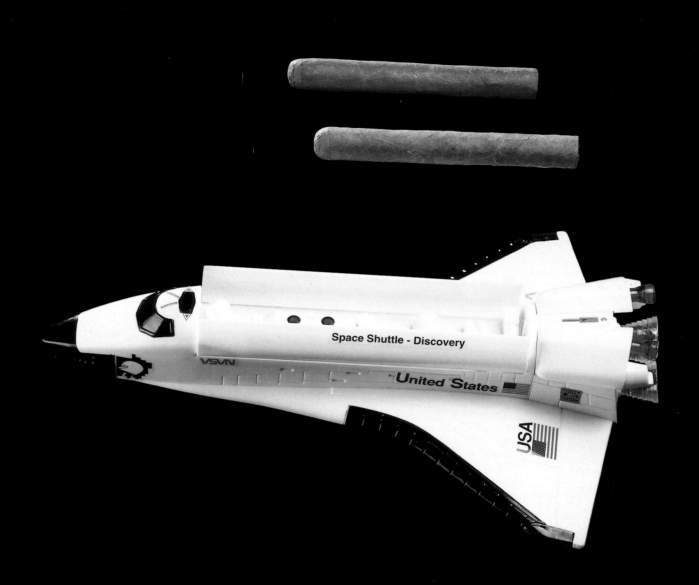

In 1989, NASA secretly deployed two Super Stratosferos into deep space to study the effects of long-term weightlessness on tobacco products. The findings remain mysteriously confidential on orders from the Agency for Tobacco and Firearms.

A religious experience.

Epilogue

Dateline: Los Angeles. The near future.

The members of the Anti-Tobacco Lobby (ATL) were jubilant when they received the news that the Supreme Court had ruled in their favor, banning the classic ballad "Smoke Gets in Your Eyes" from public airwaves and ordering that all copies of the recording be burned. In a public statement, the ATL claimed, "The interests of all those who are incapable of independent thought are the beneficiaries of this exciting development. We cannot allow a song as beautiful as this to be open to misinterpretation, encouraging lovers and others to cause secondhand (or in the case of cigars, previously used) smoke to fog the eyes of the innocent." A spokesperson for the Acceptable Behavior Coalition (ABC) added, "This is a giant step for the New Order. It brings us closer to a master race and a final solution."

Acknowledgments

Grateful thanks are due to those who generously helped create this book: Dan Sundstrom, Kay Tornborg, Harvey Markowitz, Frank Cardoza, Peter Hoffman, Frank Piccolo, Dennis Clark, Carole and Barry Kaye, Alice Lloyd George, Bob Blakeman, Kosh, Robert Mundy, Michael Tuchner, and Ralph de Blanc...who kindly supplied the cigars.

Bibliography

A Life of Leaves. Ramon Cortez. Miami: Esperanza Books, 1954.

A Churchill Before Breakfast. Arturo Cortizone. Miami: Esperanza Books, 1960.

Cuba, My Cuba. Enrico Fabulare. Boston: Heart & Sole Publishing, 1936.

Collecting Cigar Boxes. Larry Pippick. Petaluma, Calif.: 2 Speed Press, 1980.

Ashes to Ashes. Adia Muchacho. Havana: Havana University Press, 1932.

A Churchill After Lunch. Arturo Cortizone. Miami: Esperanza Books, 1963.

Sexing Tobacco Plants. Dr. Luis Cohen-Goldsmith. San Francisco: Trimesta Books, 1990.

Mysteries of the Cigar. Guido Enzo. London: Rexall & Smythe, 1980.

Smoke 'Em If You Got 'Em. Harry Corfu. Little Rock, Ark.: Timberland Tree Press, 1988.

The Double Corona Mystery. Eileen Prinn. New York: Paperthin Books, 1987.

A Puff's Enough. Ferdinand Ortega. Havana: Aragon Publications, 1950.

Aroma Therapy: Health Through Smelling. Dr. Angelo Cartahena. Cheyenne, Wyo.: Wyoming University Press, 1987.

Foggy Days, Smokey Nights. Duane Hickey III. Lafayette, La.: Buckeye Books, 1969.

A Churchill Between Courses. Arturo Cortizone. Miami: Esperanza Books, 1968.

Holy Rollers: Cigar Production in the Nunnery of Ste. Miracle. Vatican City: Ecumany Books, 1970.

Blend Your Own: A Beginner's Guide. David Van Halen. Halifax, Nova Scotia: Scotiabooks, 1980.

Directory of Cigar B.S. Henri de Villeneuve. New York: Caliber Press, 1995.

A Churchill Before Dying. Arturo Cortizone. Miami: Esperanza Books, 1976.

Aftertaste. Donald Halitosa. Stratford, England: Bard Student Library, 1988.

The Black Humidor Murders. Priscilla Hatchard. Lafayette, La.: Buckeye Books, 1969.

Credits

17 . . . . . . Toy Zeppelin: Courtesy LJP Props.

18 . . . . . . Set dressing: Courtesy LJP Props.

19 . . . . . Litho steamship: Courtesy Kay Tornborg.

20-21 . . . . Set dressing: Courtesy LJP Props.

23 . . . . . . Starship model: Courtesy LJP Props.

26 . . . . . . Bisque nudies: Courtesy Kay Tornborg.

27 . . . . . . Blender: Courtesy LJP Props.

28 . . . . . . Grinder: Courtesy LJP Props.

29 . . . . . . Model chaise and shade: Courtesy Kay Tornborg.

30 . . . . . . Flower pot: Courtesy LJP Props.
             Picture Frame: Courtesy Kay Tornborg.

32 . . . . . . Juke box: Courtesy LJP Props.

33 . . . . . . Erte figure: Courtesy The Franklin Mint.
             Rings: Courtesy Kay Tornborg.

35 . . . . . . Saddle: Courtesy Kay Tornborg.

36 . . . . . . Refrigerator: Courtesy Kay Tornborg.

38 . . . . . . Accessories: Courtesy LJP Props.
             Gun: Courtesy Kay Tornborg.

41 . . . . . . Boots: Courtesy LJP Props.

44-45 . . . . Figures: Courtesy LJP Props.
             Easel: Courtesy Kay Tornborg.

46 . . . . . . Pipe: Courtesy LJP Props.

49 . . . . . . Easel: Courtesy Kay Tornborg.
             Ash tray: Courtesy Robert Mundy.
             Fan: Courtesy LJP Props.

54 . . . . . . Ink bottle: Courtesy LJP Props.
             Pen accessories: Courtesy Kay Tornborg.

55 . . . . . . Book, figures and train: Courtesy LJP Props.

58-59 . . . . Green sward: Courtesy Kay Tornborg.

61 . . . . . . Elephants, pyramid and sand: Courtesy LJP Props.

63 . . . . . . Green sward: Courtesy Kay Tornborg.

64 . . . . . . Model tower: Courtesy LJP Props.

65 . . . . . . Model White House: Courtesy Alice Lloyd George.

68 . . . . . . Book, ashtray and condom: Courtesy LJP Props.

69 . . . . . . Model Empire State Humidor: Courtesy LJP Props.

70 . . . . . . Weights: Courtesy LJP Props.

71 . . . . . . Roulette accessories: Courtesy LJP Props.

72 . . . . . . Candle holder: Courtesy LJP Props.

73 . . . . . Kiddie Kampers toy: Courtesy Kay Tornborg.

74 . . . . . . Artisan toys: Courtesy LJP Props.

75 . . . . . . Couch: Courtesy Kay Tornborg.
             Television: Courtesy LJP Props.

76 . . . . . . Automated model: Courtesy Off The Wall,
             Melrose Avenue.

77 . . . . . . Meat cleaver: Courtesy Kay Tornborg.

78 . . . . . Vat of goo: Courtesy Robert Blakeman Studios.
             Figures: Courtesy LJP Props.

82 . . . . . . Egyptian sarcophagus: Courtesy Sylvia and
             Barry Kaye, Museum of Miniatures.

83 . . . . . . Figures and cart: Courtesy LJP Props.

85 . . . . . . Model horse: Courtesy LJP Props.

86 . . . . . . Glass tumbler: Courtesy LJP Props.

87 . . . . . . Toy hydra: Courtesy LJP Props.

88-89 . . . . Flat figures: Courtesy Kay Tornborg.

93 . . . . . . Figures: Courtesy LJP Props.

94-95 . . . . Ash trays: Courtesy Picolo Pete's.

96 . . . . . . Model bed: Courtesy Kay Tornborg.

97 . . . . . . Figures: Courtesy LJP Props.

99 . . . . . . Toy theatre: Courtesy Kay Tornborg.

106 . . . . . Model Space Shuttle: Courtesy LJP Props.

107 . . . . . Figures: Courtesy LJP Props.

108 . . . . . Record player and disc: Courtesy LJP Props.